Thomas Osmond Summers, Horace W. Wightman

Waukeenah's slave

Thomas Osmond Summers, Horace W. Wightman

Waukeenah's slave

ISBN/EAN: 9783744739245

Printed in Europe, USA, Canada, Australia, Japan

Cover: Foto ©ninafisch / pixelio.de

More available books at **www.hansebooks.com**

WAUKEENAH'S

SLAVE.

A LEGEND
BY
T. O. SUMMERS.

WITH 18 ORIGINAL ILLUSTRATIONS.
DRAWN BY,
HORACE W. WIGHTMAN

CARLTON REGAND,
PUBLISHER.
1160. BROADWAY.
New York.

WAUKEENAH'S SLAVE.

.

List of Illustrations.

LEGEND.

It is said that a short time ago an Indian Chief appeared on the Streets. of St Augustine accompanied by an old negroman.

       After viewing the wonderful Ponce de Leon Hotel, and the ancient Fort, he tried to sell the slave; but upon being informed that slavery was a thing of the past, he offered the negro his freedom, and returned alone to his home in the Everglades.

WATCH TOWER SAN CARLO
1656.

On the blue Matanzas frowning,
With its proud Castillian crest,
All its dark embrasures crowning
Looks San Marco
from the west.

There it stands, a strange exotic,
In this land of palms and sands;
Planted by a race despotic,
Reared by shackled Indian hands.

Once the sheen of
Moorish lances
Glittered from those
gray old walls;
Spaniards wove their
weird
romances
In those dark
coquina
halls.

At its' feet all cramped
and
crouching,
Lies the ancient sea girt town;
Eltrich houses,
gables touching,
Roofs of tileings
rude
and
brown

Through those gates
        now old
                and crumbling,
Proudly pranced the Knights
                of Spain,
Now the
        ox team
                slowly rumbling,
Enters from the
                sandy
                        plain.

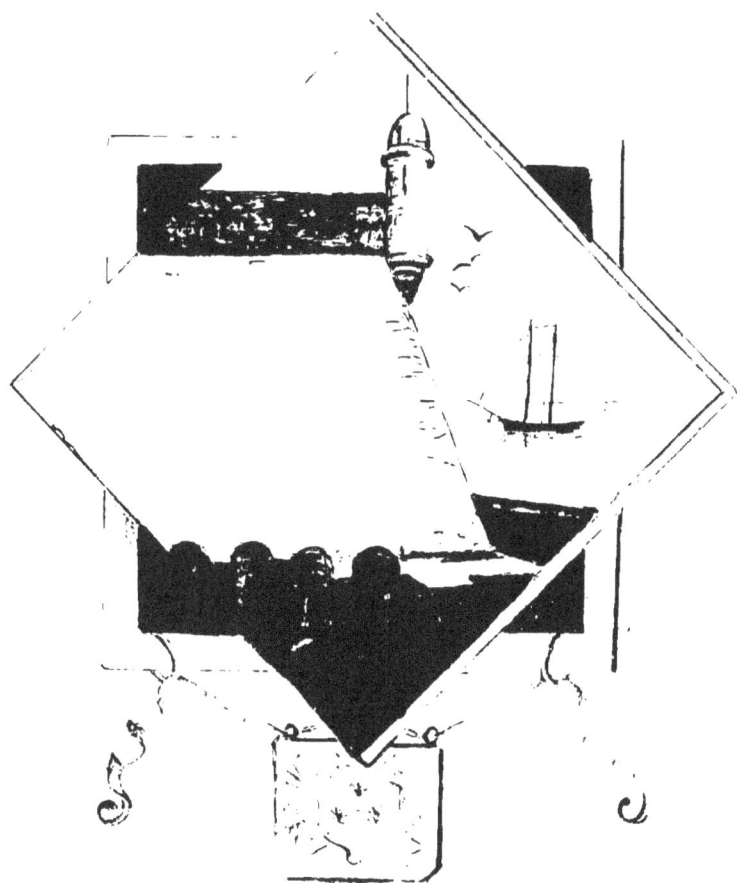

Garden wall and
            quaint piazz
Mauritanian portals low.
Old Cathedral,
            Market plaza,
Tell the tale of long ago.
Spain has lost her tyrant
            power,
And her flag no more
            is seen
Flying from that grim
            old tower,
Once the pride
            of
            Augustine.

Oer'it floats
    Columbia's banner,
Emblem of the
      free
        and
         brave;
Guarded by no mailed
       retainer,
Minion, vassal,
      serf
      or
       Slave.

Far within this land
                 of flowers,
In the gloom of forest shades
Indian braves dwell
                 'neath the bowers
Of the pathless Everglades.

There was one,
                 a tawny giant,
Last of all his scattered
                 tribe,
Remnant of a race
                 defiant,
Néer subdued,
                 nor won
                       with bribe.

By the still Miami River
Roamed Waukeenah child of doom,
And his steps had wandered never
From his fathers forest home.

All his kindred brave had perished
All had been the whitemans foe
And within his heart he cherished
Hate that burned with hellish glow.

Once as silently he pondered
O'er the fate that doomed his race,
And with wild conjecture wondered
Who would come to fill his place;

Suddenly a great emotion
Swept across his heaving breast,
As a storm breaks on the
                    ocean,
When its waves are all
                    at rest.

Near a spring whose
                crystal flashes
Ripple to the tideless wave
By the campfires smouldering
                ashes,
Sat a captive Indian slave
Years had flown since from
                the battle
He had been as booty brought
In the days when like
                dumb cattle
Afric's sons
            were sold
                and
                    bought.

Kindred ties had long been broken,
And his rude uncultured tongue,
Only Indian words had spoken,
Only Indian songs had sung.

As he sat, Waukeenah turning
Thus, with frowning visage spoke
'Rise Lenoir my heart is burning
To behold this pale faced folk.

I have heard the wondrous story
Of their crowded cities great
Of their deeds on fields of glory
Where my fathers met their fate.

Foes they are to both our races
Mine has perished by their hands
I would look into their faces
I would view their fertile lands."

By Welaka's still
meandering,
On through hammock
marsh
and plain,
After long and weary
wandering.
They behold
the
mighty
main

* Former name of St. John's River,
meaning chain of lakes.

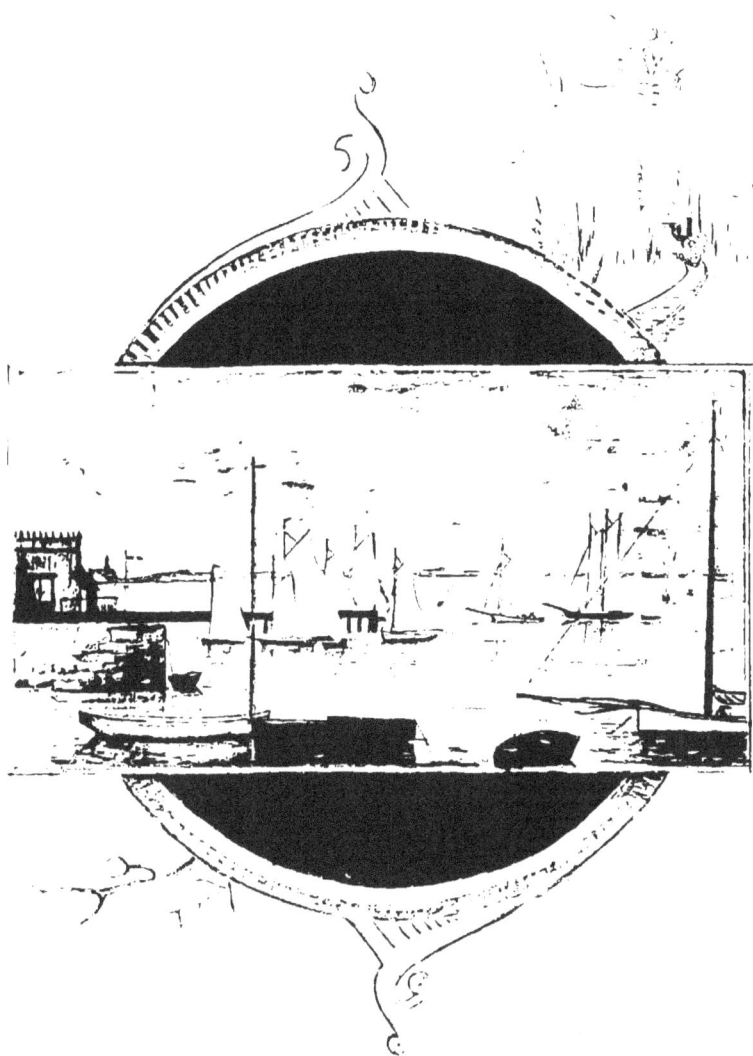

Saw they then the
       harbor teeming
With the sails of moving
               ships,
Heard the throbbing
           engines screaming,
And great wonder
           sealed
               their
                 lips.

From the
old cathedral
pealing,
Rang the chimes out on the air;
Oer Waukeenah came a feeling
Of a strange and deep despair.

Round them both there soon assembled,
Those who would their mission know,
And Waukeenah's great form
trembled,
As he spoke in accents
slow;

"I have come to view this city
To behold your works of art;
But I ask not love or pity
From the white man's
            murderous heart.
Once my fathers brave,
            defended
With their lives this
            lovely land;
With its soil their
            blood
            is blended,
Dying by your
            conquering
                        hand.

28

I am now content to perish;
Since your glory   .
                    I have seen,
Naught there is for me to cherish,
But the thought
            of what has been.

By the banks of that lone
                    river,
In my far off forest home,
I shall dwell, unknown
                    forever,
And await my
            peoples
                doom.

Take this slave,
      twas here I
            found him,
Take him at the price ye name,
With your
            shackles
            ye have bound
                  him
To a life of toil
            and
                  Shame:

Scarcely had the words
           been uttered,
When a negro bowed with years,
Trembling towards
           Waukeenah
                tottered,
And his eyes were
           filled with
                tears.

With a voice all filled
                with feeling,
To Waukeenah thus
                he spoke.
And his frame
          all bent and reeling,
With a strange emotion shook:
Savage see my head is hoary,
And I soon shall be at rest;
But my heart leaps
                at your story,
And a wild hope fills
                my breast.

Streaming from
yon ancient
tower,
See that starry banner wave,
Neath its folds, no man
hath power
God's own image
to
enslave

I have felt the curse
                    of slavry,
  Under which my people groaned,
  Yours have perished in their
                        bravry,
Dying for the land they owned.

But a brighter day has broken,
And its bars of massy light
Are the bright and peaceful token,
Of the triumph of the right.
Open then thy long closed vision,
And the present glory see
Thou canst find a noble mission
'Neath the banner
                    of the free.

"No Waukeenah answered
                    sadly,
Not for me the white man's
                    art;
See these pulses beat too madly,
I have still a savage heart

Ye may take this poor old
                    creature,
Tell him of his changed estate,
It may please his servile
                    nature,
I shall choose my fathers fate".

Then Waukeenah
           proudly
                turning
From the plaza moved away,
With a heart all filled
           with yearning
   For his wild home,
           far away.

As he stood there
          dumb with wonder
Looked the old man
          on Lenoir,
And he cried in voice
          of thunder
"I HAVE SEEN THAT
          FACE
               BEFORE."

Then there came an
                    inspiration
Of a strange and wondrous light,
Dawning like a new creation,
On the dark of nature's night.

"It is he! in every feature,
I can well his Kinship trace;
Naught deceives the eye
                of nature
Son, behold thy
            father's face!

* * * * * * * * * * * * *

In the west, the sun
was setting;
Ponce de Leon's windows
flamed;
And a weird fantastic fretting,
With a purpling splendor
streamed.

Through its gorgeous halls
and spaces,
Moved the masters
of the earth,
But not one of all their faces
Told what real joy
was worth.

A ray of heavenly light
was beaming
From two faces on that eve;
Through their hearts
such peace
was streaming,
As the world
can
never
give.